Savannah
impressions

photography by Robb Helfrick

FARCOUNTRY
PRESS

In memory of Spencer Cason—a gentleman from Savannah.

Right: Across the Savannah River to the dome of City Hall.

Title page: The Granite Steps Inn on Gaston Street.

Front cover: Springtime in Forsyth Park.

Back cover: Stormy sunrise over Tybee Island.

ISBN: 1-56037-223-0
Photographs © Robb Helfrick
© 2002 Farcountry Press

Created, produced, and designed in the United States
Printed in Korea

Right: Southern traditional goes international in a plate of fried green tomatoes with corn relish, with polenta, and shallot crostini.

Below: Corinthian capitals ornament a Whitaker Street home.

Inside the Green-Meldrim House on Macon Street, one of the finest examples of Gothic Revival architecture, and open for public tours.

Above: Face-to-face with a blue crab.

Left: South End Beach on Ossabaw Island.

Fort McAllister State Historic Park, which includes a restoration earthwork fort like the one built here during 1861-1862.

The family parlor in Juliette Gordon Low Birthplace on Oglethorpe Avenue,
childhood home of the Girl Scouts founder and now a museum.

Right: Aerial view of Factors Walk, where cotton brokers worked when King Cotton ruled.

Below: Dogwood blossoms tell of spring's arrival.

Above: An Ossabaw Island alligator, calm and content for now.

Facing page: One of the island's live oak–lined lanes provides a passageway for a purposeful pig.

Above: Tybee Island in the Atlantic Ocean provides a refreshing getaway for Savannahians.

Facing page: The Masonic Lodge in the Cotton Exchange is the oldest continuously operating one in the nation, dating from 1734.

Above: In the historic district, Foley House Inn bed and breakfast is in a restored Victorian townhouse.

Left: River Street's shops, galleries, and restaurants are a tourist Mecca beside the Savannah River.

Above: Detail of the Forsyth Park fountain.

Left: Sunset at low tide on the Isle of Hope.

Maritime forest habitat at the edge of a Skidaway Island marsh.

Facing Monterey Square in the historic district.

Above and right: All Savannahians are Irish every March 17, one of the city's largest festivals.

Facing page: Telfair Square in its spring glory.

Above: In Chippewa Square.

Facing page: Spanish moss trims a Skidaway Island live oak.

Above: Tybee Island's current lighthouse dates from 1866, but the first one was built here in 1736.

Left: Eerie lighting glows on the Ogeechee River near Savannah.

Above: The "Silence" monument watches over Confederate graves in Laurel Grove North.

Right: The 1871 Mercer House on Monterey Square was built, but never occupied by, Confederate General Hugh Mercer, and is a private family home.

Above and facing page: Fort Pulaski, on Cockspur Island at the mouth of the Savannah River, was completed in 1847, seized by Confederate troops on the eve of the Civil War, and still bears signs of the thirty-hour bombardment by Union cannons in 1862.

Above: Parlor of the Ballastone Inn, a historic-district bed and breakfast in a restored 1838 house.

Facing page: City Hall was completed in 1905.

Below: A great egret in Savannah National Wildlife Refuge, across the Savannah River from the historic district.

Facing page: Sailing from Sunbury south of Savannah, these shrimp boats supply the city's tables.

Above: A featured exhibit in the converted train shed that houses the Savannah History Museum is this 1890 Baldwin locomotive.

Right: Savannah is rightfully famous for its azalea displays, as seen here on Jones Street in the historic district.

Above: Evening begins at the Hamilton-Turner Inn, in the historic district.

Facing page: Preparing for a dinner cruise of the Savannah River aboard a replica 19th century paddlewheeler.

Above: Ebeneezer Creek Swamp is not far from the city.

Facing page: Fort McAllister at nearby Richmond Hill is an example of Confederate earthwork fortifications.

Above: Classic Southern cuisine is on the menu in this former mansion.

Facing page: In early spring, azalea blossoms add to Forsyth Park's charm.

Above: The Forsyth Park Fountain is styled after the one in Place de la Concorde, Paris.

Facing page: The Mercer House entrance.

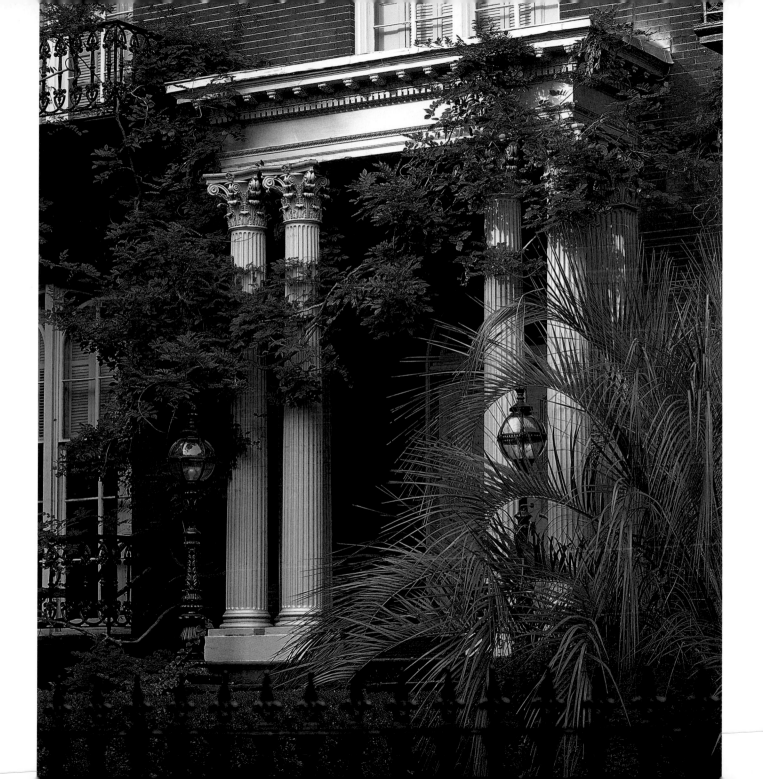

Above: Kayaking is one way to enjoy the Georgia coast.

Right: Marsh reflections on Ossabaw Island.

Cathedral of St. John the Baptist, dedicated in 1876, underwent extensive restoration at the turn of the 21st century.

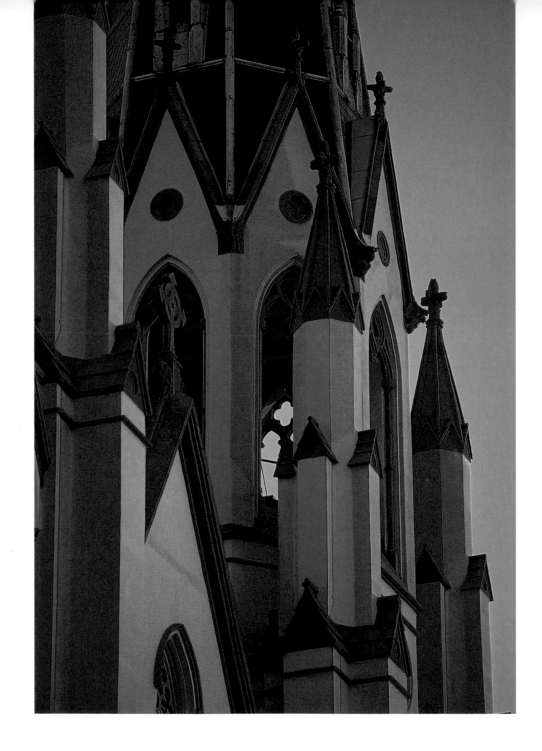

A sunset view of the Talmadge Bridge on the Savannah River.

Right: Cotton bolls ready for picking.

Below: Beloved symbols of the South, in Monterey Square.

Facing page: Church detail in Chippewa Square.

Above: Narrated carriage tours are an excellent way to learn about the historic district.

Facing page: Reynolds Square is among the twenty-two open spaces that survive from twenty-four created when Savannah was platted in 1733.

Above: The parlor of the Eliza Thompson House, an inn housed in an 1847 Federal-style mansion on Jones Street.

Facing page: Intriguing design in the historic district.

Above: Dogwood blossoms.

Right: Some of the nation's finest funerary sculpture—including this portrait named "Gracie"—is in Bonaventure Cemetery.

Facing page: Forsyth Park.

Above: A modern shrimpboat at nearby Sunbury.

Facing page: Independent Presbyterian Church, built in 1890 as a replica of the church on this site from 1815 until an 1889 fire, was where Woodrow Wilson married Ellen Axson.

An early-morning stroll on the Atlantic.

Above: Colonial Park Cemetery served Savannah from 1750 to about 1850.

Facing page: Enjoying Whitefield Square on a spring day.

Above: Forsyth Park's Confederate monument.

Facing page: A view from Greene Square.

Savannah National Wildlife Refuge at dusk.

Afternoon tea and evening libations are offered at the Magnolia Place Inn.

Above: This great blue heron calls the Savannah National Wildlife Refuge home.

Facing page: Azaleas are everywhere in the spring.

A tall ship docked on the Savannah River.

Above: Along Gaston Street.

Right: In Chippewa Square, this statue portrays Georgia Colony—and Savannah—founder James Oglethorpe.

Facing page: The Green-Meldrim House.

Above: Orleans Square.

Facing page: Factors Walk shopping.

Above: This mythical protector of the Cotton Exchange dates from 1886.

Facing page: Restored warehouses make up today's City Market arts, shopping, and entertainment district.

Above: Tybee Lighthouse at last light.

Facing page: A luxuriance of azaleas.

ROBB HELFRICK lives in Atlanta, and specializes in location photography for editorial and corporate clients. His photographs have appeared in *Atlanta Magazine, Sierra, Town & Country, Sky, Hemispheres, National Geographic Traveler, National Parks,* and *Travel Holiday* magazines, as well as in many books and calendars. He was the sole photographer for the Fodor travel guide *Georgia*, for the guidebook *The Civil War in Georgia,* and for *Georgia Simply Beautiful* (Farcountry Press, 2002). He is a recipient of the Leonard Foote Memorial Award for Excellence in Conservation Photography, which is given by the Georgia Wildlife Federation. Along with photographing the American South, with emphasis on the foremost travel cities, he currently is documenting his favorite wild place in *Georgia: The Okefenokee Swamp.*